Written by Georgia Amson-Bradshaw

Illustrated by David Broadbent

W

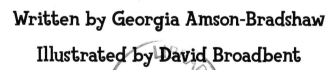

Franklin Watts
Published in paperback in Great Britain in 2020 by The Watts Publishing Group
Copyright © The Watts Publishing Group, 2019

Produced for Franklin Watts by
White-Thomson Publishing Ltd
www.wtpub.co.uk

Series Editor: Georgia Amson-Bradshaw
Series Designer: David Broadbent
All Illustrations by: David Broadbent

Printed in Dubai

Franklin Watts
An imprint of
Hachette Children's Group
Part of The Watts Publishing Group
Carmelite House
50 Victoria Embankment
London EC4Y 0DZ

An Hachette UK Company
www.hachette.co.uk
www.franklinwatts.co.uk

Facts, figures and dates were correct when going to press.

CONTENTS

Look out for this little book symbol to find definitions of important words. Other definitions can be found in the glossary on page 30.

What is equality?

Equality is the idea that everyone is worth the same. Each human being should have the same opportunities, rights and treatment as everyone else. Equality means that no one is better or more deserving than anyone else simply because of who they are.

Human rights

Our human rights are things we are allowed simply because we are human. They include things like the right to life, to live freely and not as a slave, and the right to be treated equally by the law.

History of an idea

The belief that everyone is equal hasn't always been around. In many countries during the medieval times (from the fifth to the fifteenth century), it was accepted that some people had more rights than others. At the top of society was the king, whose position was believed to be chosen by God.

A new politics

In time, people began to challenge this idea. In many countries, the idea that everyone is equal became a key belief that changed how their governments worked. 'Liberty, Equality, Brotherhood' was made France's national motto in the nineteenth century when Emperor Napoleon III (1808–1873) was exiled.

The United States Declaration of Independence, signed in 1776, begins "We hold these truths to be self-evident, that all men are created equal". Nowadays, this idea is written into international agreements, such as the Universal Declaration of Human Rights.

Equality today

Despite these agreements, there is a lot of inequality around the world. Chances are that how you experience life and how much money you have will be affected by a number of things.

These include where you live, whether you are born a boy or a girl, who your parents are, whether or not you have a disability and the colour of your skin.

Inequality around the world

With over seven and a half billion people in the world, all living incredibly different lives, it can be hard to understand what inequality really means. So let's start by imagining there are only **100** people in the world.

11 of them are living on just $1.90 US dollars (£1.40) each day for all their food, clothes and housing. What could you buy with £1.40?

1 single person has half of all the money in the world.

22 people don't have a home that keeps them properly warm, dry and safe.

11 people would not be getting enough food to eat each day.

14 people would not be able to read or write.
What would be different in your life if you couldn't read or write?

Unfairly shared

There are enough resources in the world to go round. For example, we already grow enough food to feed everyone a healthy diet. The problem is that resources are unfairly shared. Some people have much more than they need, while others don't have enough.

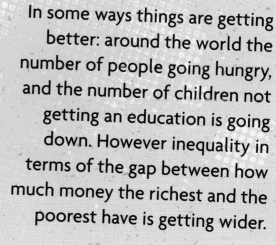

In some ways things are getting better: around the world the number of people going hungry, and the number of children not getting an education is going down. However inequality in terms of the gap between how much money the richest and the poorest have is getting wider.

We are all equal...
or are we?

Inequality isn't just about how much money or things we have. It's about whether we all have the opportunities to live a full life, to get a good education and be treated with respect and dignity, free from discrimination.

Discrimination

The unfair treatment of a particular person or group, based on some aspect of who they are.

Gender inequality

Women and girls make up half of the world's population. But gender inequality means that girls are given fewer opportunities and freedoms compared to boys.

Everyone has a right to education, but particularly in poorer countries, the reality is that many girls still get denied the chance to go to school, or are made to leave school at a much younger age than boys. After school, women around the world often earn less than men for doing the same work.

Race and ethnicity inequality

We use the word race to describe people's physical features, such as the colour of their skin and the shape of their faces. Ethnicity describes someone's cultural characteristics, such as their language, religion and ancestry.

Around the world, people's races and ethnicities affect their life chances. For example, in the UK, people who are not white and British find it harder to get jobs and so are 12 per cent more likely to be unemployed.

Ability inequality

Globally, 15 per cent of people have some kind of disability, such as being blind or deaf, having learning difficulties or trouble moving around.

People with disabilities have the same needs and rights as everyone else: to learn, to have a social life and get jobs, earning them money and building self-esteem. But fewer than 20 per cent of disabled people are employed.

why is equality important?

If you weren't allowed to go to school, but instead you had to go to work every day doing a dirty job such as searching through a rubbish dump for bits of plastic, how would you feel?

And if you got paid less than other people for doing exactly the same work, just because of who you are, how would you feel? You'd probably think it was pretty unfair.

A better life

One reason why equality matters is fairness. But you might wonder, 'Isn't it only the poorest people who would benefit from greater equality, and not people who are already well-off?', After all, they might end up with less money or having to compete harder for opportunities! In fact, a more equal society is better for everyone, even the well-off, for several reasons.

The evidence

People have done many studies on countries around the world. Some countries are much more equal than others, with a smaller difference between the poorest and the richest, and better opportunities for girls, people with disabilities and people of different ethnicities.

In places that are more equal:

★ There is less violence. In the most unequal societies, the number of murders is five times higher. Violence is often caused by people feeling looked down on or disrespected. In equal societies, this happens less.

★ Everyone is happier. People trust their neighbours more, and are less worried about crime and violence.

★ People are physically and mentally healthier. In the most equal societies, people live longer and feel better. And this is even true for the richest people in those places, not only the poorest.

In what other ways do you think a more equal society might be better?

Does equal always mean fair?

Look at these two pictures. In the first scene, the children are being treated equally. They each have one box to stand on.

But is this fair? The tall boy doesn't need a box to see over the fence. The little girl can't see at all!

Compare the top picture to this picture. The boxes have been rearranged, and everyone can see.

Each kid has what they need, rather then being treated exactly the same. **The outcome is fair.**

OK, but how do kids standing on boxes relate to bigger issues of inequality?

Inequality in action

Only five per cent of the heads of the world's biggest companies are women. This is not because women are only five per cent as intelligent or hardworking as men.

The low number of women in powerful jobs has many causes, such as people not seeing women as leadership material, or women having to take time out of their careers to raise children, while men are not expected to look after kids at home.

One idea to help address this inequality is for businesses to only consider women candidates when hiring for some roles.

But hang on – isn't it important to treat everyone equally when they are applying for a job?

But, if it's harder for women to get powerful jobs due to reasons beyond their control, then unequal treatment in certain circumstances could create a fairer outcome overall – just like with the boxes.

What do you think?

Sweetie-sharing challenge

If you were in charge, how would you share out the world's wealth? Look at this picture. All the world's wealth is being shown here as 100 sweets. Each jar represents 20 per cent of the world's population.

This jar is the poorest 20 per cent of people

Second-poorest 20 per cent

Middle 20 per cent

0 sweets

0.25 sweets

1 sweet

Does this look fair to you? How would you share the sweets differently?

Draw this

Using a piece of plain paper and some colouring pens, draw five jars to represent the world's population broken up into five groups. Inside each jar, draw coloured circles to show the number of sweets that you think each group deserves.

You have 100 sweets to share out – no more or less! How many sweets will you put in each jar?

Second-richest 20 per cent

Very richest 20 per cent

Would you put the same number of sweets in every jar? Or do you think there are reasons why some people should have more sweets than others?

9 sweets

89.75 sweets

Remember, your jars represent people who are doing all sorts of different types of work. The sweets are the world's money. Would you give more sweets to people who do difficult and dangerous jobs, or not? What about people who can't work due to illness?

The game of inequality

Find a die and two counters, and play this game with a friend. Each player follows one path. Taking turns, roll the die to see how many coloured spaces to move forward. Will you beat the odds? First one to the finish line wins!

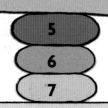

PLAYER ONE START HERE!

1. Your name is James. You live in the UK. Your family love you very much, and they are quite rich.

2

3

4. Your parents hire a nanny, who teaches you to read. Move forward three.

5

6

7

8. At primary school your parents can afford music lessons and sports trips for you. Move forward a space.

9

10. You go to a top private secondary school. Your parents also hire a tutor to give you extra help. Move forward two.

PLAYER TWO START HERE!

1. Your name is Amira. You live in the UK. Your family love you very much, but they are quite poor.

2

3

4. Your parents work two low-paid jobs each. No one has time to read with you. Miss a go.

5

6

7

8. Your home is damp, so you fall ill a lot and miss days at school. Move back a space.

9

11 12

13. With your grades, musical ability and sporting success you get into a top university. Move forward a space.

14

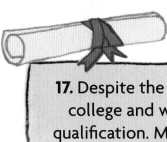

17. Despite the difficulty of juggling college and work, you pass your qualification. Move forward a space.

18 19

20. You apply for a lot of jobs after college, but no one calls you back. At interviews people explain they want people who have already got relevant work experience.
Miss a go.

16

15. While at college you have a waitressing job to help pay rent at home. It makes you tired. Miss a go.

21

22

14

23. You find a job. Congratulations!

13. You get accepted into a good university, but it's far away from home in an expensive city. You decide to go to the local college and live at home. Miss a go.

FINISH LINE!

23. You get promoted to a high paying role. Congratulations!

12

11

22

21

10. Your secondary school isn't great, but you work hard. You get a mix of B's and A's. Move forward a space.

20. One of your friends' dads works for a big bank. He knows you, so he recommends you for an internship after you graduate. Move forward three.

19

18

15. At uni, you make a lot of friends who are also from well-off families. Move forward a space.

16

17. You graduate with a good degree. Move forward two spaces.

PICTURE THIS

Try this drawing challenge. Take a plain piece of paper and some colouring pencils. Draw pictures of the following people.

1. A brain surgeon

2. A politician

3. A childminder

4. A nurse

Underneath each picture, decide on a name for them, and write that down too. **Don't read the bottom of the page until you have completed the challenge!**

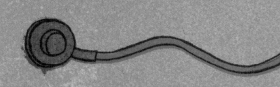

Have you drawn the pictures yet? Don't read on until you have!

OK, so who did you draw? Chances are you drew men for the first two, and women for the second two. Over our lives, we start to pick up assumptions about what sorts of jobs are appropriate for men and women.

We develop stereotypes about what boys and girls are like. These stereotypes tell us that powerful jobs, such as being a politician, or highly skilled roles, such as being a brain surgeon are done by men. Jobs that involve caring for people are done by women.

Stereotype

A belief that we unthinkingly have about people because of some element of who they are, such as 'girls like dolls' or 'boys like cars'.

Seeing stereotypes

What other assumptions do you think people make about boys and girls, and how they should behave? Have you heard any of these phrases?

'Boys don't cry.'   **'Man up!'**

'That isn't ladylike.'
                    'You run like a girl.'

How do you feel if someone says one of these things to you?

Look at these pictures of children's toys. What do these toys and phrases say about how boys and girls should behave? Write down a list of words that go along with the stereotypes for boys and girls. For example;   boys = strong, tough, sporty.
                    girls = weak, pretty, gentle.

How might these stereotypes be harmful for both girls AND boys? What do you think are the biggest problems that stereotypes cause?

LET'S ROLL

Do you remember being little and not being able to reach things on shelves, or needing a booster seat to sit at the table?

As a little kid it can be difficult to reach or access certain places or things, because the size of the furniture and everything else isn't designed for young kids: it's designed for adults. Once you grow bigger, that stops being a problem. But what about people who continue to find the environment isn't designed for them?

Challenge:

Find a large object with wheels, such as a big wheely suitcase, a trolley or pram. Now try to complete the following tasks:

★ Go for a walk, such as from your house to the shops or a bus stop

★ Walk around a large building, such as your school

★ Go to the toilet

★ Join in a game in the playground with friends.

BUT:
You must **ALWAYS** follow the **RULES** ...

THE RULES

1. You cannot LIFT the wheely case or trolley, not even a few centimetres!

2. No tipping it so that only some of the wheels are touching the ground. All the wheels must be on the ground the whole time.

3. You must be holding onto and pushing the case at all times. For example, you are not allowed to let go of the case to open a door. You must try and open the door while holding onto and pushing the case.

What do you notice about the built environment as you try to wheel your case around?

It's difficult to simply wheel a large object around many spaces. What if you had to wheel yourself around? Very often the built environment is not designed so that people in wheelchairs can get into and around them. Wheelchair users don't have equal access to those places.

Can you think of other ways that people with disabilities might be denied equal access and equal treatment? Can you think of some solutions?

Built environment

The human-made spaces we live in every day, including buildings and parks, and the furniture walls, doors and steps inside them.

Making Change Happen

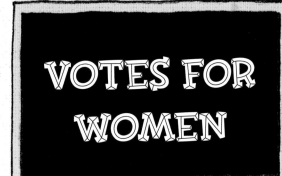

When problems are really big, it can seem like nothing can be done about them. But people can change things. A little over a century ago, women couldn't vote anywhere in the world.

A woman's place

For much of history, women have been treated as inferior to men. For example, in Europe and the USA before the nineteenth century, everything a woman owned became the property of her husband once she married.

Universities did not accept women students, and while men could divorce their wives for being unfaithful, women were not allowed to divorce their husbands – and they certainly couldn't vote.

Voting victory

Since being given the vote in Saudia Arabia in 2015, women now have the same voting rights as men around the globe. This is down to the hard work of millions of tireless campaigners, some of whom gave their lives to make the world fairer. However, gender inequality means fewer women are involved in politics than men.

Political power

The first country in the world where women won the right to vote in national elections was New Zealand. Suffragette Kate Sheppard organised massive petitions to parliament and pressured them into passing a bill in 1883 that gave women the right to vote.

However, women in New Zealand were still prevented from standing for political office. The first country to allow women to stand as political candidates was Finland, in 1906. In 1907, the first female members of parliament were elected there.

The various women's rights movements in countries around the world used many different techniques to advance their cause; from petitions and protest marches, to radical direct action, such as smashing windows and even setting fire to empty buildings.

Profile: Malala Yousafzai

Malala grew up in the Swat Valley in Pakistan. It was an area controlled by the Taliban, a violent political group who follow a very extreme version of Islam. The Taliban don't believe in equal rights for women. They are not allowed to go to school, and can't even leave their houses without being accompanied by a male relative. This is very different to how most Muslims, such as Malala and her family, practise their religion.

Helped by her dad, who was a human rights activist, Malala started a blog aged 11 where she wrote about her experiences, and argued for her right to go to school. She appeared on television, and became well known around the world. She was nominated for an International Children's Peace Prize.

When she was 15 years old, she was shot in the head by a Taliban gunman on her way to school. She was very ill, but she survived and slowly recovered in hospital. She and her family moved to the UK.

A year after her attack, Malala gave a speech at the United Nations about the right of all girls to get an education. In 2014, she was awarded a Nobel Peace Prize for her activism. She was the youngest ever recipient, at 17 years old. She started the Malala Fund, an organisation that funds girls' education projects around the world and advocates for girls' rights to learn.

Despite almost losing her life for her beliefs, Malala continues to speak out for equality.

Activate!
Make equality infographics

Facts and figures in the news about inequality can often sound like meaningless numbers. Showing the same information visually using pictures or infographics can help give people a better understanding of the size of the problem.

Infographic
A way to show data or information in the form of a picture.

Look at how the following statistics have been shown visually using infographics. Can you see how pictures have been used to show the numbers in a more interesting and easily understood way?

The richest 1 per cent of people have more money than the other 99 per cent put together.

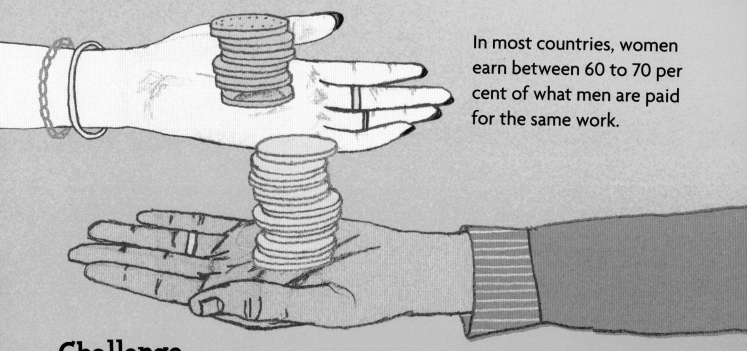

In most countries, women earn between 60 to 70 per cent of what men are paid for the same work.

Challenge

Draw a set of posters featuring your own infographics that you have designed, showing either the facts already illustrated on this page, or any of these statistics:

✳ In the USA, the typical white family has thirteen times more money than the typical black family.

✳ The richest eight men in the world have the same amount of money as 3.6 billion people.

✳ In 80 per cent of countries, the gap between richest and poorest is getting wider.

Put your posters up somewhere they will be seen to help educate people about the huge level of global inequality.

organise!
Hold an equality day

Beginning to tackle any really big problem starts with people being aware of its causes and effects. A fun way to help people understand equality better is to hold an equality day. Here are some ideas for activities you could include – but try to come up with your own ideas too!

Board games

Look at the board game on pages 16–17. Put this out for people to play, or design and make your own inequality game. Why not research what life is like for someone born in a poor country, and base your own board game around that?

You can also take existing board games and change the rules. For example, put out the game Monopoly, but have one player start the game already owning a lot of houses. Have different players earn different amounts as they pass Go.

sports day

Run some classic sports day activities, such as an obstacle race, or an egg and spoon race. But put more obstacles in some people's tracks than others, or give some people a much larger spoon.

Explain how these differences represent the real life differences that people face. Come up with some other variations on classic games.

cake stall

Hold a cake stall, but make the slices of cake for girls only 70 per cent as big as the ones for boys – even though they cost the same. Then swap over so the boys get smaller portions!

What other ideas can you come up with?

Glossary

activism promoting a cause and working for social change

built environment the human-made spaces we live in every day, including buildings and parks, and the furniture, walls, doors and steps inside them

direct action a kind of protest that uses non-violent but attention-grabbing actions, such as holding marches and blocking roads

discrimination treating someone unfairly because of assumptions you've made without really knowing them

equality the idea that everyone is worth the same and no one is better or deserves more than anyone else simply because of who they are

ethnicity a cultural background that you share with a large group of other people

human rights things that everyone must be allowed, no matter what country they live in – for example, the right to education and to be treated equally by the law

inequality when people are not equal and some are treated better or have more simply because of who they are

infographic a way to show data or information in the form of a picture

internship paid or unpaid work experience with a company or organisation, usually for a set period of time

medieval describes the period in history from CE 476 to 1492, known as the Middle Ages

motto a short saying that sums up a belief or a chosen way of doing things

petition a written document, often signed by lots of people, asking someone with power to do or change something

political office a position in the government that someone is voted into by the public

stereotype an overly simple, untrue idea that many people have about a group – for example, that men are bad at cooking and cleaning

United Nations an organisation with many member countries that works for world peace

Universal Declaration of Human Rights an international document that lists and describes the rights that everyone in the world should have

Further information

What is feminism? Why do we need it? And other big questions
Louise Spilsbury and Bea Appleby (Wayland, 2017)
This book explores feminism and the ongoing struggle for women's equal rights. It encourages you to think for yourself about tough questions and challenge stereotypes and traditional beliefs.

What is gender? How does it define us? And other big questions for kids
Juno Dawson (Wayland, 2017)
In this book you can learn more about different gender identities, and how people can be stereotyped and treated differently because of their gender.

This kid can fly: it's about ability (NOT disability)
Aaron Philip and Tonya Bolden (Balzer and Bray, 2016)
In this memoir, Aaron Philip, a fourteen-year-old boy with cerebral palsy, shares his honest and often funny stories about having to overcome physical difficulties, poverty and other challenges.

Websites

www.youtube.com/watch?v=G3Aweo-74kY
Watch a classroom experiment about gender inequality and stereotypes linked to different jobs that people do.

www.youtube.com/watch?v=w6dnj2IyYjE
An introduction to the idea of intersectionality, which means thinking about how different parts of someone's identity come together and how that may affect their life.

www.youtube.com/watch?v=QBWrF-R272s
Young people react to inequality and discrimination in different experiments, exploring ideas of unfairness and solutions to make things fair for everyone.

www.youtube.com/watch?v=2KlmvmuxzYE
A short video about privilege and how people with privilege tend not to recognise their unfair advantages.

www.un.org/en/universal-declaration-human-rights
Download a pdf of the universal declaration of human rights here.

Note to parents and teachers: every effort has been made by the Publishers to ensure websites are suitable for children, that they are of the highest educational value, and that they contain no inappropriate or offensive material. However, because of the nature of the Internet, it is impossible to guarantee that the contents of these sites will not be altered. We strongly advise that Internet access is supervised by a responsible adult.

Index